East Kilbride
Then & Now
David Pettigrew

The Maxwells of Calderwood were fond of adorning their estate with follies. As well as the miniature Craigneath Castle, there was also the Hermitage and the Fairy Well, both on the Rotten Calder south of Calderwood House (just east of the modern houses of Inch Keith). The well, seen here, was probably built in the 1840s and featured a stone slab built around a spring emerging from a cliff face. The poem inscribed on the slab read:

> *If thy Spirit is Pure as this crystal spring,*
> *Stranger, drink its waters, and fearlessly fling*
> *The tiny cup in the bright fairy well*
> *Its magic for Thee has no fatal spell.*
> *But enchantment falls on all around*
> *Above, below, tis hallow'd ground,*
> *And Truth lies hid in this mystic well*
> *With power each secret thought to tell.*
> *Then pause! stranger, pause! for if evil dwell*
> *In thine heart, Dare not quaff*
>   *The Fairy Well!*

Text © David Pettigrew, 2024.
First published in the United Kingdom, 2024,
by Stenlake Publishing Ltd.,
54-58 Mill Square,
Catrine, Ayrshire,
KA5 6RD

Telephone: 01290 551122
www.stenlake.co.uk

ISBN 9781840339185

The publishers regret that they cannot supply copies of any pictures featured in this book.

Acknowledgements

The author wishes to thank Ian Bushnell for his kind permission to take the photograph of Old Craig Mill.

Further Reading

The books listed below were used by the author during his research. Only *Old East Kilbride* is available from Stenlake Publishing. Those interested in finding out more are advised to contact their local bookshop or reference library.

Francis H. Groome, *Ordnance Gazetteer of Scotland*, 1886.
Yvonne Hillyard, 'The architects of East Kilbride's Development Corporation and the post-war New Town' in *The Dictionary of Scottish Architects*, Historic Environment Scotland, 2017
Robin and Susan Hunter, 'Craig Mill, Eaglesham', *Renfrewshire Local History Journal* Vol. 17, 2013
Stuart Marshall, *Old East Kilbride*, 1994
Bill Niven, *East Kilbride From Old Photographs*, 2015
Bill Niven, *East Kilbride Through Time*, 2009
The Topographical, Statistical and Historical Gazetteer of Scotland, 1847
Daily Record
Evening Times
'Calderwood Country Park' (guide), South Lanarkshire Leisure and Culture, 2013

alfredgilletttrust.org
assets.savills.com
thecastleguy.co.uk
East Kilbride Old Parish Church: https: ekopc.org.uk
historicenvironment.scot
letslookagain.com
menziesaviation.com
networkrailmediacentre.co.uk
National Museums Scotland: nms.ac.uk
oldglasgowpubs.co.uk
railscot.co.uk
rampantscotland.com
Calderglen and Calderwood Castle History (facebook)
East Kilbride Heritage Group (facebook)
Scottish agricultural implement makers (facebook)
'East Kilbride – The Making of a Town' (1996):
    www.youtube.com/watch?v=N5M_S80uMMQ

Introduction

Recognising the need for the redistribution of the populations of the industrial centres of central Scotland and also for new housing after the Second World War, the New Town Act was passed in 1946. The following year the village of East Kilbride was designated Scotland's first New Town. This was intended to be a new kind of community, housed in high quality modern homes, separated from Glasgow by a green belt, and given its own amenities and employment opportunities through encouraging businesses and manufacturers to base themselves in an area with excellent transport links. In the decades to follow, East Kilbride expanded to encompass all of these, with the population rising to over 75,000 at the time of the last census.

Development was steered under the aegis of East Kilbride Development Corporation which existed for 50 years until it was disbanded and the town came under the control of South Lanarkshire Council. Some local people feel that, as a result, the fortunes of the town have declined since then as in its heyday the Corporation had built a strong local economy basically from scratch, creating 35,000 jobs. It had also attracted well-known architects to design prestige buildings for its public amenities, including Basil Spence (Duncanrig School) and Alexander Buchanan Campbell (Dollan Baths, now the Aqua Centre).

Before all this, East Kilbride was a small community based around a centre – now known as 'the Village' – containing coaching inns and a parish church. The wider parish had been settled from at least the twelfth century and there was a school by the 1590s and several castles in the area. Farming was the main source of employment and the town was made a burgh of barony, with four fairs per year and a weekly market, in the early eighteenth century. There was a cotton mill and a brewery by the 1820s and a post office by 1838. The railway arrived in 1868. By 1945 the village had become quite large, a population of nearly 2,500 being served by 40 shops.

Before 1947 there were three factories making agricultural equipment. New Town status brought the National Engineering Laboratory at Birniehill and then, in 1953, the Rolls Royce factory at Nerston. By the end of the 1950s, 5,000 people were being employed in 23 new factories. This industrial prosperity waxed and waned over the following decades with closures and job losses being balanced by new openings and opportunities. Besides Rolls Royce, other world-famous manufacturing names to have provided employment over the decades have included Schweppes, Motorola, Decca, JVC, Linn, Seagate, Fuji and Jeyes.

There has perhaps been a tendency to focus the history of East Kilbride on the 50 years of the Development Corporation, but the town has continued to grow since this was wound up, with a great deal of new housing appearing in recent years. It is now 75 years since it became famous as a New Town, a moniker that is now part of the town's history rather than its defining trait. As the photographs in this book show, East Kilbride continues to adapt to the times as the years roll on.

Main Street, looking north towards its junction with Old Coach Road. The house facing the camera is the Old Toll House, now the premises of the Lamont Dental Clinic. This was built in the late eighteenth century for the collection of tolls on a new turnpike road running from Ayrshire to Edinburgh, which was partly funded by the Stuart family of Torrance House. The toll road from Glasgow to London also ran through the village and there was another toll house on Graham Avenue.

For many decades in the twentieth century the Old Toll House housed the local police station. On the immediate right is the front garden wall of the Parish Council Chambers, built in 1913 and now a private dwelling. The fence on the left of the old photo belonged to the coach house that was established in 1783 and is now the Torrance Bar and Restaurant.

The gala queen procession being escorted by a pipe band down Main Street is about to cross the railway bridge (the wall of the bridge is still partially *in situ* though the site of the railway in this immediate vicinity is taken by car parks off Old Mill Road). The photo probably dates from after 1924 when the Union Petroleum Products Co., a London-based company, was renamed the Redline Motor Spirit Co. This later became Redline-Glico. The Redline brand was well-known into the 1950s; the garage buildings had been cleared by then.

In the background of both these photographs are the gates to East Kilbride High School, which opened in 1880 and was known as the old Village High School (it was later officially designated as East Kilbride Junior Secondary School). It closed in 1984 and became the base for South Lanarkshire College until 2008 when Tulloch Homes acquired the site, demolished the school building, and built apartments on it. The junction with Old Mill Road is on the right; this street was laid out after the 1890s.

Main Street, as seen from the northern end of Stuart Street in 1952. The building with the prominent chimney in the distance stood opposite the High School. This factory and the buildings immediately in front of it, which belonged to a garage, have been replaced by flats and a car park.

Most of the buildings in the foreground of the old view are still standing. The Union Bank of Scotland merged with the Bank of Scotland in 1955; the local branch is now in Princes Mall.

Hunter Street, seen here in a photograph taken over 105 years ago, remains intact. The high roof of East Kilbride Old Parish Church is to the left of the two-storey house at the far end of the street. The church was built by James Pollock in 1774/75 and the steeple, with its crown belfry, was added in 1818. This houses the current bell, installed in 1881 to replace the 1818 original. The adjacent Old Hall was erected in 1912 (the New Hall opened in Glebe Street in 1974).

At the end of Hunter Street, directly in front of the church and left of the house facing the camera, is the Montgomerie Arms. Converted into a pub in 1957, this was originally a coaching inn and dates back to 1656. In front of the Montgomerie Arms, and visible in the old photo in front of the house facing the camera, is the Loupin On Stane, a mounting block that was installed in 1719 to allow for easier mounting and dismounting from horseback.

A 1920s photo of Parkhall Street, with the Old Parish Church in the distance. The fencing on the right bounded open space which has since been taken by the sheltered housing of Ladybank Court.

Except for the church, all of the buildings visible in the old photo have long since been replaced by flats and housing. The prospect of the church is also now somewhat marred by the addition of the monolithic Hunter Community Health Centre which looms behind the steeple. This was opened in 2015 at a cost of £19.6 million.

Kittoch Street, viewed from West Mains Road. The West Kirk on the left was formed in the eighteenth century when a portion of the Parish Church congregation broke away in protest at the appointment of a new minister who was not their choice. The congregation called themselves the 'East Kilbride Congregation of Relief' and in 1791 contracted a local mason, John Cairns, to build this church at a cost of £900. A manse built behind the church was replaced by the church hall in 1930.

The West Kirk was refitted and reroofed in 1866. In the latter half of the nineteenth century the congregation joined the United Presbyterian Church which then merged with the Free Church of Scotland to form the United Free Church. In 1929 the U. F. Church buried the hatchet and amalgamated with the Church of Scotland. The house on the right of the old photo is now the site of South Lanarkshire Council's Lindsay House 1st Stop Accommodation and, as seen above, the original Kittoch Street today forms an access road to the car park next to the West Kirk.

East Kilbride Station was opened by the Caledonian Railway Company in 1868. There was a goods shed here, seen here on the right, which was later used by a scrap merchant until it was demolished as part of the redevelopment of the station around 1990. The potential benefits of the village's railway links was one of the reasons why East Kilbride was chosen as the site for Scotland's first New Town. The houses of Kirktonholme Road, among the first local authority houses built in the 1940s as part of the New Town, are on the left. A major aspect of New Town development, the building of modern houses, initially fell behind schedule, with only 801 being completed within the first six years due to shortages of building materials.

The New Town house-building rate recovered and from the mid-1950s around a thousand new homes were being built annually. The trend for building new homes has more or less continued ever since. The flats of Kirkton Gate now occupy the area right of the station while, on the left, the fields that stretched down from Kirktonholme Road have been filled by the station car park and the houses of Kirktonholme Gardens. The name 'Kirktonholme' is derived from the Victorian house of 'Kirkton Mains Holme' (later marked on maps as 'Kirktonholm Mains') which still stands on Dryburgh Lane to the west of the Kirktonholme area.

This view was taken in 1952 and shows some of the first homes of New Town – Park Terrace is in the foreground – bordering those of the old village. The High School is in the background on the left and the Old Parish Church is on the right.

The hill on which these photographs were taken is the site of the Dollan Baths, later renamed the Dollan Aqua Centre. Named after the former Lord Provost of Glasgow and chairman of East Kilbride Development Corporation, Sir Patrick Dollan, the A-listed baths building was designed by Alexander Buchanan Campbell, whose plans were influenced by Japanese architecture. The baths opened in 1968 as Scotland's first 50-metre swimming pool and underwent a £9 million refurbishment between 2009 and 2011.

These early New Town-era houses photographed in 1952, probably when newly-built, are on Carrick Road in Market Hill, north of the Main Street and Old Coach Road.

Although the houses have been reroofed, the street remains remarkably similar 72 years later.

Priestknowe Roundabout, East Kilbride.

Priestknowe Roundabout lies just south-east of the old village. Left of centre, in front of the trees, is the 1937 memorial to the Hunter brothers, William and John, who were born at Long Calderwood near East Kilbride in 1718 and 1728 respectively. Both went on to have distinguished careers in London as anatomists. William was also a leading obstetrician and a collector of books, manuscripts, coins, minerals and zoological specimens; he bequeathed his collection to the University of Glasgow and it became the basis of the University's Hunterian Museum and Art Gallery. The 1838-built Wellbeck House stands behind the trees, a contrast to the mid-twentieth century flats of Nos. 21-31 Main Street opposite it, just right of centre.

The Three Bears sculptures now adorn the roundabout itself but, besides the removal or replacement of some street furniture, not much else has changed over the last 60 years: even the sign for Churchill Avenue is still *in situ*!

Shopping Centre, East Kilbride   PN4983

Constructed on the lands of Mid Murray Farm (see page 31) south of the old village, these shops on Cornwall Way were the first to be built for the New Town. Along with the Stuart Hotel at the far end, they opened in 1959 as part of a square of connected offices, shops and a post office, bounded by Cornwall Street to the north and Princes Street to the south – an area that is roughly an eighth of the size of the shopping centre that has extended from it since.

Remarkably, all of these units are still in use and the only change to the view is the removal of the hotel (now a gap site; the large building that can be seen above is the Civic Centre across Cornwall Street, opened in 1968) and the introduction of the bus station concourse in the foreground, replacing the original car park.

The buildings of Princes Street and Princes Square were completed in 1962. Towering in the background is Norfolk House which from 1966 was home to East Kilbride Development Corporation before it moved to Atholl House in 1975 (from inception in 1948 it was based in Torrance House). Like the Corporation, both of these buildings have now gone.

Princes Street and Princes Square have since become Princes Mall, part of the existing shopping centre – known locally as 'The Centre' – which is the largest in Scotland and comprises several malls: The Plaza (started in 1971), Princes Mall (1984), Southgate (1989), Olympia (1990), Princes Square (1997), Centre West (2003) and The Hub (2016). The malls are all now undercover, an outcome rather different from the intentions of the original planners.

Centre Roundabout and Hotel, East Kilbride   PN4981

The Stuart Hotel with the sunken gardens of Centre Roundabout in the foreground. The hotel was opened by Scottish and Newcastle Brewers in 1959 and named after the Stuart family, owners of Torrance House from the early seventeenth century. Over the decades the hotel was a favourite venue for weddings with its grand ballroom, cocktail bar and plush Tartan Room.

The Stuart Hotel eventually closed and the building became derelict. Sadly, it was demolished in 2013 and there is still a gap site where it stood. An exact replication of the original view is now impossible due to plantings on the near side of the roundabout. On the right of both views is the fire station on Cornwall Street.

HIGH MURRAY SCHEME, EAST KILBRIDE   D 1407

Over the 50 years of its existence, East Kilbride Development Corporation built 24,000 homes. The first of these were completed on Lindsay Road in 1949 but others soon followed at the neighbourhoods of East and West Mains, Westwood and at The Murray, houses of which are seen here in 1956 (the flats of Naysmyth Bank are at the top of the hill). The Murray Primary School, the first school for the New Town, had opened just two years earlier. The Murray One scheme of 206 houses and 98 flats, covering 23.1 acres, was designed by architects Robert C. Stones. They won a 1952 Saltire Award for their work and, overall, the Corporation's planners won or were commended for Civic Trust and Saltire awards twelve times in the 1950s and 60s.

High Murray and Mid Murray were names of farms on whose land the new houses were later built. These were owned by brothers Robert and John Wiseman. Robert started a modest horse-and-cart milk delivery business to 120 local homes in 1947 and this eventually developed into one of the biggest milk supply businesses in Britain. New flats on the opposite side of The Murray Road from the houses now occupy the spot from which the older photograph was taken. The empty foreground area of land was later taken by the industrial units of Bramah Avenue, James Watt Avenue and Naysmyth Avenue and Place.

Calderwood House stood on a site near the west bank of the Rotten Calder Water ('Rotten' is derived from a word for 'Red', the colour of the ironstone over which the river flows). The site is in woodland very close to the houses of Ellisland Drive. Often known as Calderwood Castle, it was built in 1773 to replace a Scots Baronial-style tower house which had been constructed by the Maxwell family in the early to mid 1400s. The house, seen here in March 1928, was extended in a Gothic Revival style in the 1840s but in 1904 the estate was sold to the Scottish Co-operative Wholesale Society, which used the land for agriculture.

The house became a billet for troops in the Second World War and afterwards fell derelict. East Kilbride Development Corporation bought the estate in 1947 and what was left of the house was demolished in 1951. Only some parts of the walled driveway terrace at the front of the castle remains (the castellated pillars in the older photo can just be made out on the left here). Calderglen Country Park comprises the old Calderwood and Torrance estates. The park opened in 1982 with a visitor centre based in the seventeenth-century Torrance House, which also lies just west of the Rotten Calder though further south.

Craigneath Castle, Calderwood Estate.

Craigneath Castle was built by the Maxwells of Calderwood north-east of Calderwood House, across the Rotten Calder, sometime between 1750 and 1845. Despite the appellation of 'castle', it was actually a relatively small two-storey building which was part-accommodation for servant staff and part-folly, distinguished with a tower that gave a vantage point across Calderwood Glen. A footbridge across the river connected the two properties.

The castle has been more or less completely torn down and reduced to rubble.

After Calderwood Castle was taken over by the Scottish Co-operative Wholesale Society in 1904 the grounds were opened to the public. This platform was built by the Caledonian Railway to serve visitors coming by train, though they still had some distance to walk as the platform was to the north-west of Calderglen, opposite the houses which stand just east of the junction of Flemington Road and Stoneymeadow Road.

Calderwood Glen had regular services until 1924, thereafter being used for excursion trains. It closed in 1939 and the track was later removed. As this photo shows, the line is still discernible amongst the farmland but there is no trace left of the platform.

MAINS CASTLE, EAST KILBRIDE   B 5871

Lying to the north-west of the old village, Mains Castle – seen here in 1952 – was the stronghold of the Lindsay family who built it in the latter half of the fifteenth century. The last owner from that family apparently had to sell the estate to pay off debts. Supposedly, he was a very cruel man who once ordered one of his servants to be drowned for displeasing him and he eventually died a pauper in one of his old tenant's barns. Whether this is true or not, what is known is that the castle began to fall into disrepair from 1679 when it was damaged by the cannons of Royalist soldiers in the aftermath of the Battle of Bothwell Brig. Victorian owners put a new roof on the building in the 1880s but it collapsed during a storm in 1922.

The building remained a ruin until 1976 when the then-owner, Mike Rowan, embarked on a ten-year restoration back to its original five floors. For this he won two Saltire Awards, for the Best Restoration and Excellence in Restoration. As one of its final projects, in 1996 East Kilbride Development Corporation opened James Hamilton Heritage Park, recreating the drained loch in front of Mains Castle and building a watersports centre next to it. Trees now stand on the position from where the original photograph was taken, hence this viewpoint from a different angle.

Hairmyres Station opened in 1868 and stood in a rural location until housing estates began to surround it from the 1990s. In that decade the original station building seen here was replaced (see facing page). Work to relocate the station 600 metres to the west of the current location is taking place in 2024. This redevelopment will create a major transport interchange with park-and-ride facilities and electric vehicle charging provision and is part of East Kilbride Enhancements Project, a Scottish Government initiative to decarbonise Scotland's railways by 2035.

The station remains a major part of East Kilbride's transport development plans because just south of it is University Hospital Hairmyres. This began in 1904 with the opening of the short-lived Lanarkshire Inebriate Reformatory. With the council purchase of a nearby farm, the site became home to a tuberculosis sanatorium from 1919 and then extended into a 400-bed general hospital in the 1930s. (Treatment of tuberculosis continued with the most famous patient being George Orwell in 1946; he was in the midst of writing *1984* at the time though apparently staff confiscated his typewriter for the good of his health!) Ironically, the establishment of the New Town in 1947 did not lead to further development of the hospital, though this eventually began in the 1970s, with the hospital being completely rebuilt between 1988 and 2001 when it reopened under its current name.

The hamlet of Kittochside lies to the north-west of East Kilbride and these cottages stand where Kittochside Road meets Cairnmuir Road and Carmunnock Road. A mile or so south-west of here lies Wester Kittochside Farm, site of the National Museum of Rural Life. The farm was in the ownership of the Reid family from 1567 and the Georgian farmhouse dates from 1783.

The Reid family eventually gave the farm to the National Trust for Scotland and since 2001 it has been run as a 1950s-style farm by National Museums Scotland. The museum – originally called the Museum of Scottish Country Life – was designed by Page/Park Architects and built on newly-purchased land between 1998 and 2001.

Auldhouse E.K.

The hamlet of Auldhouse was first recorded in 1602 and in the late 1800s was noted as lying three miles south of East Kilbride, consisting of some houses, a smiddy, an inn, a shop and a school. Apart from the addition of some local authority houses and a new primary school Auldhouse is largely unchanged today, though East Kilbride is growing ever closer due to house building and is now less than a mile away.

The Auldhouse Arms has existed since around 1800. The original entrance to the inn was where the third window in from the right is today – the bowler-hatted gentleman is standing at it in the old photo. In the 1970s the inn extended into the grocers' shop to the right and in the 1990s it extended into the building to the left, which by that time had acquired an additional storey; this part became a restaurant. Meanwhile, at some point the dormers seen in the old photo were taken away (there had also once been a slate-roofed porch over the original entrance).

Hawbank Farm lay some distance to the north-west of the old village and in the mid-nineteenth century there is record of it being occupied by a Mrs Hood and owned by 'Glasgow College' (probably Glasgow University). Like many of the farms that once dotted the countryside of the parish, it has long since disappeared. As part of the New Town development, this area was cleared for industrial use with various factories being built in the 1950s, all sited well away from the New Town housing.

The farm's name lives on in Hawbank Road while the lands of the farm have become the site of the industrial units off Dixon Place; the farm buildings themselves stood on an area that is now the yard of JDP underground drainage supplies.

Old Craig Mill lies a few miles south-west of East Kilbride off the road to the hamlet of Millhall. A three-storey sandstone building, it was a grain mill standing on the north bank of the White Cart Water which powered it. Possibly built in the seventeenth century, it was first recorded on maps in the mid 1700s (a later map records it as flax mill). It was disused by 1912 though was back in operation as a grain mill by 1926 and remained in use until the 1970s.